AND WHEN I DIE

Words and Music by
LAURA NYRO

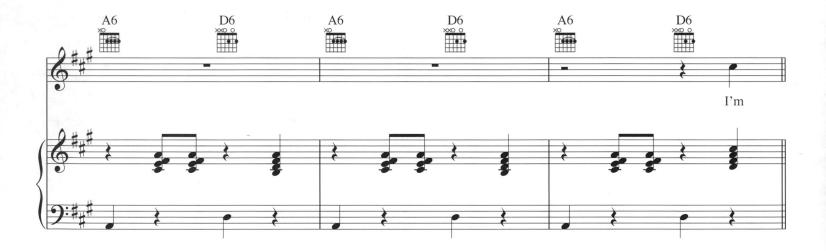

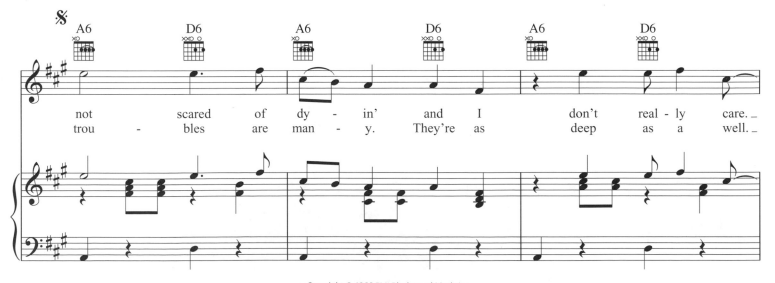

I'm

not   scared   of   dy - in'   and   I   don't   real - ly   care. _
trou - bles   are   man - y.   They're   as   deep   as   a   well. _

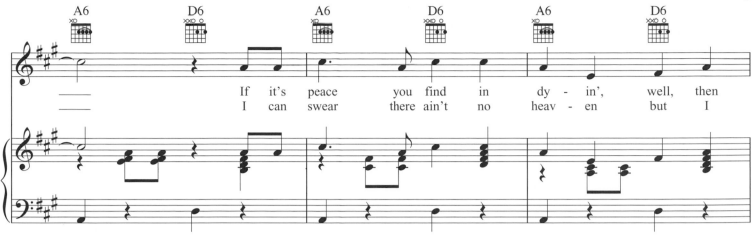

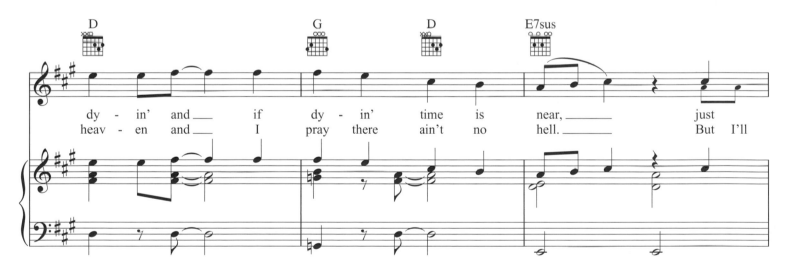

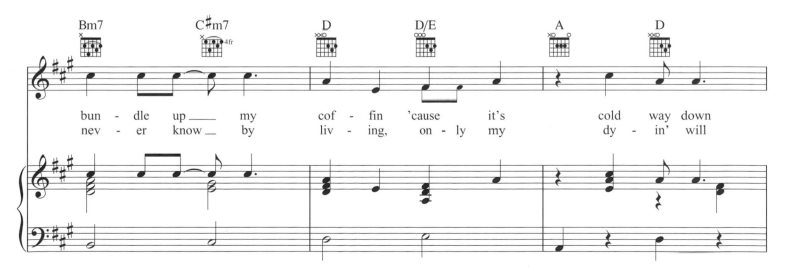

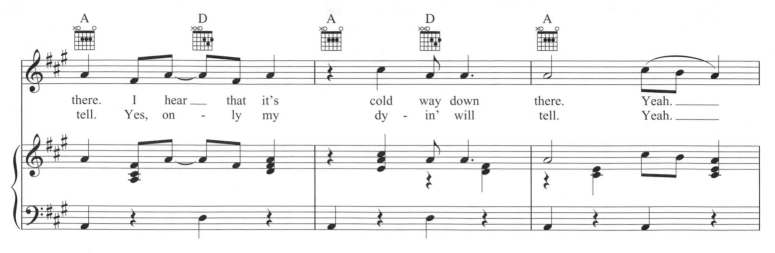

there. I hear ___ that it's cold way down there. Yeah. ___

tell. Yes, on - ly my dy - in' will tell. Yeah. ___

Cra - zy cold way down there. ___

On - ly my dy - in' will tell. ___

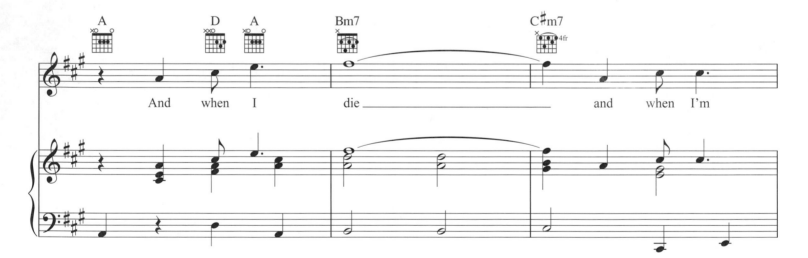

And when I die ___ and when I'm

gone, ___ there'll be one child

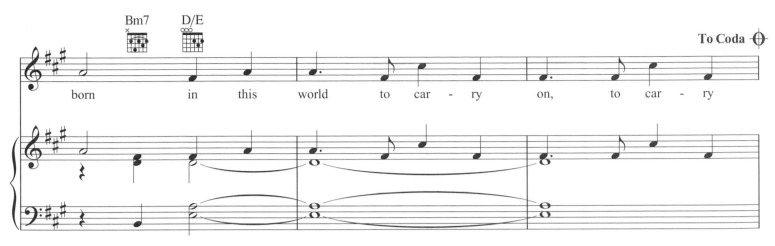

born in this world to car - ry on, to car - ry

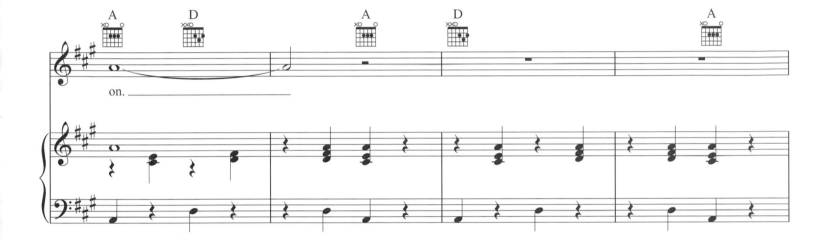

on.

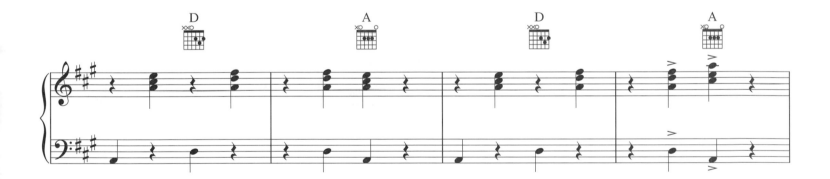

Now

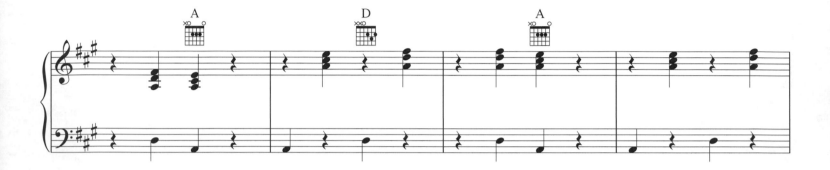

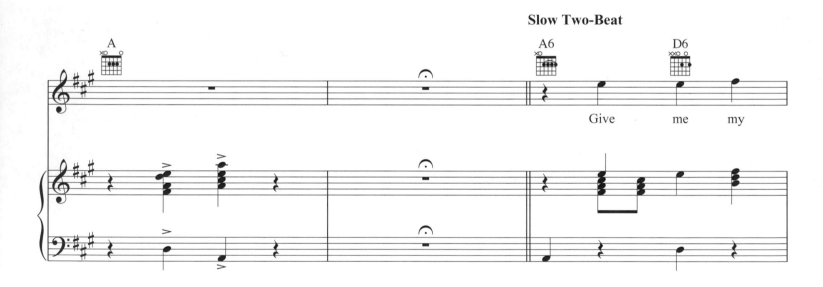

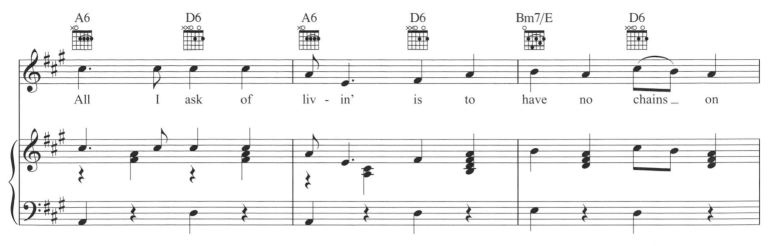

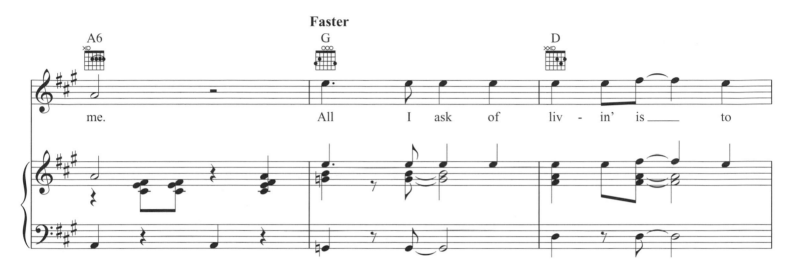

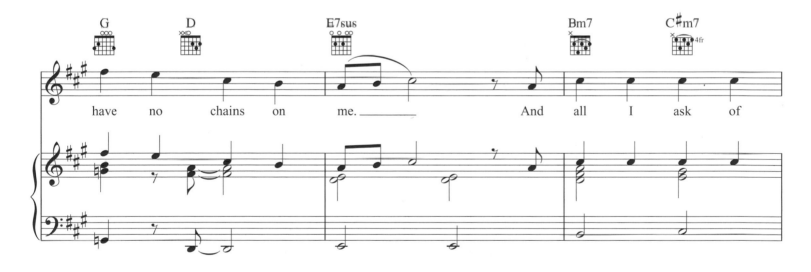

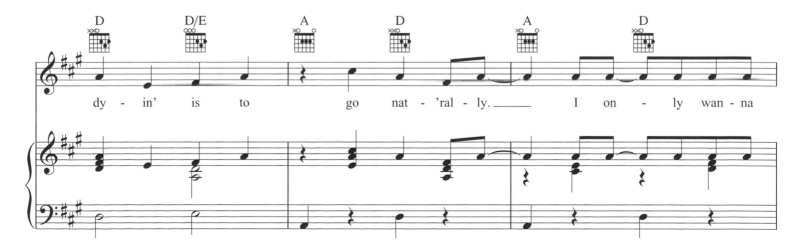

and when I'm dead, dead and gone, _____ there'll be one child

Fast

born in our world to car - ry on, to car - ry on. _____

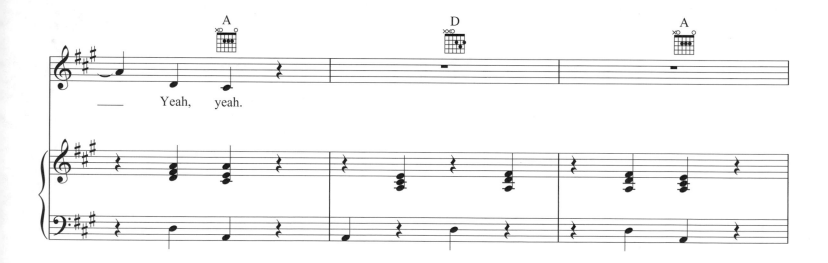

_____ Yeah, yeah.

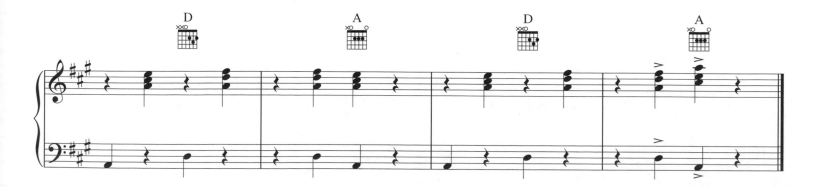

HI-DE-HO
(That Old Sweet Roll)

Words and Music by GERRY GOFFIN
and CAROLE KING

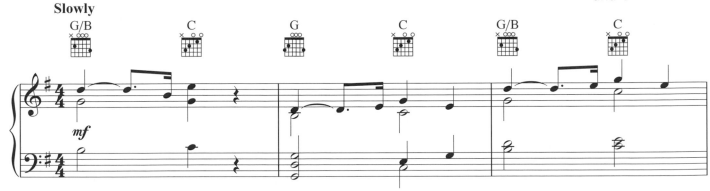

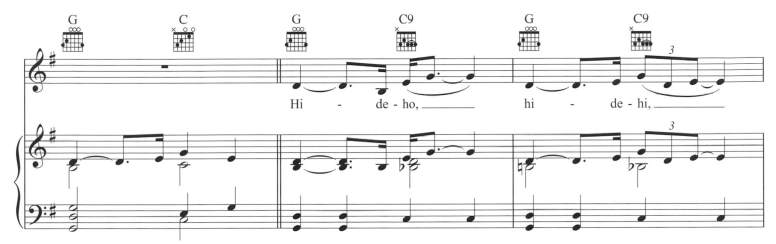

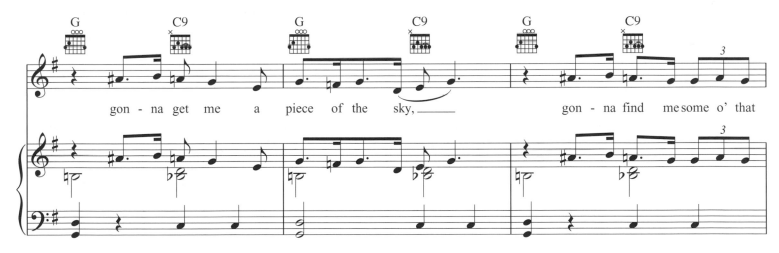

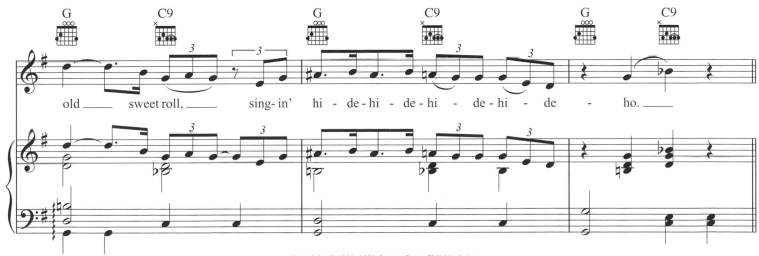

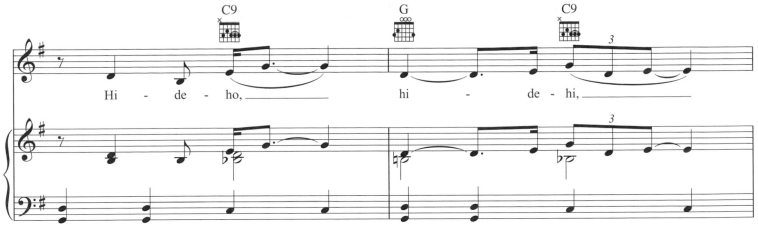

Hi - de - ho, _____ hi - de - hi, _____

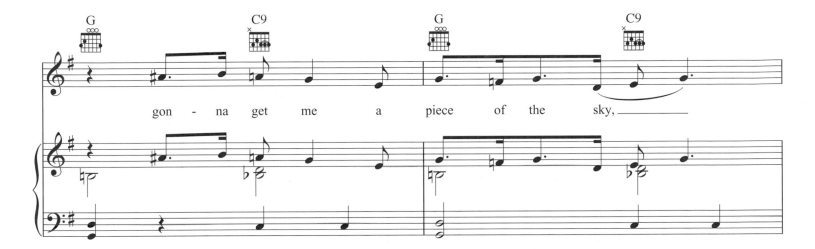

gon - na get me a piece of the sky, _____

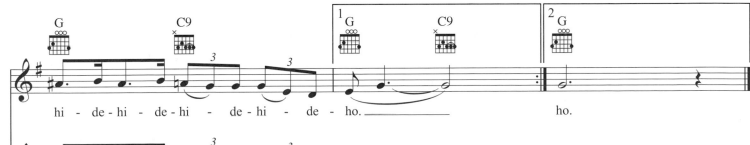

gon - na find me some o' that old _____ sweet roll, _____ sing - in'

hi - de - hi - de - hi - de - hi - de - ho. _____ ho.

GO DOWN GAMBLIN'

Words and Music by DAVID CLAYTON-THOMAS
and FRED LIPSIUS

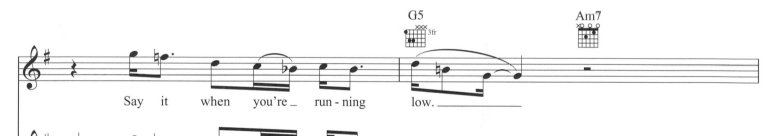

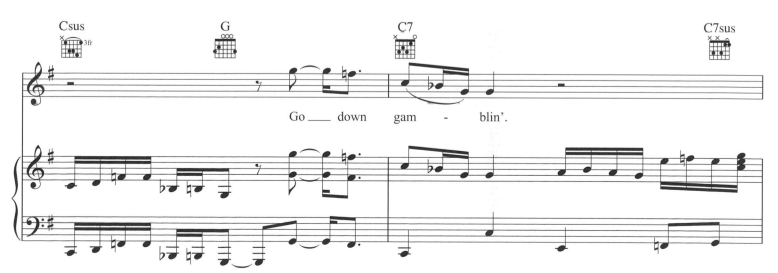

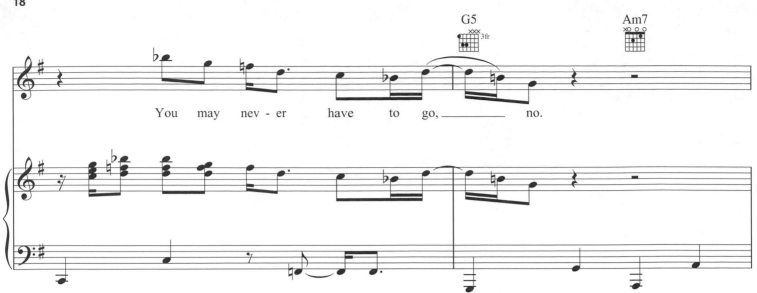

You may nev - er have to go, _____ no.

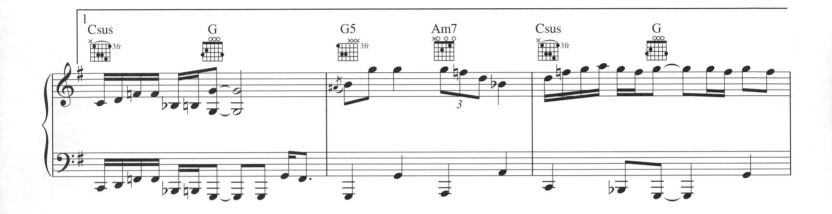

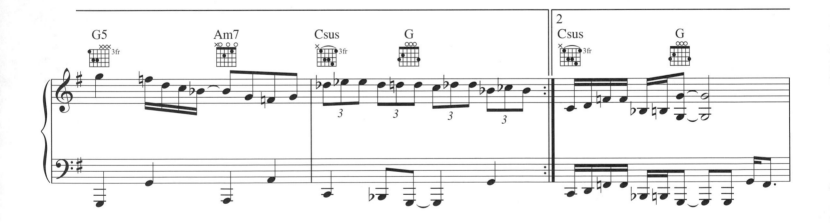

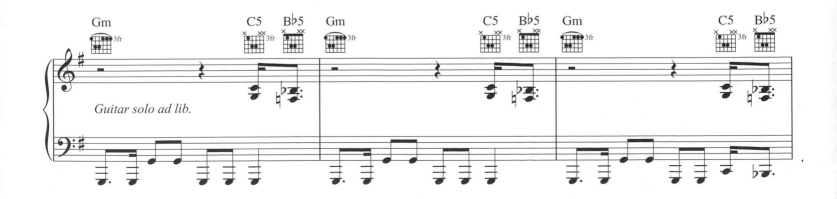

Guitar solo ad lib.

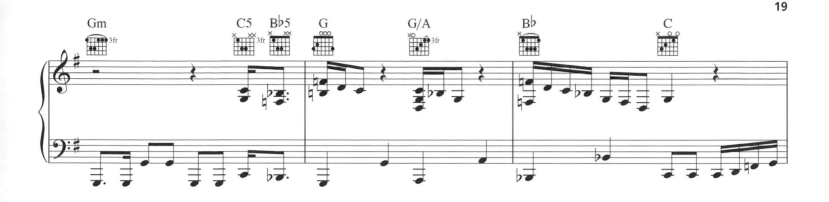

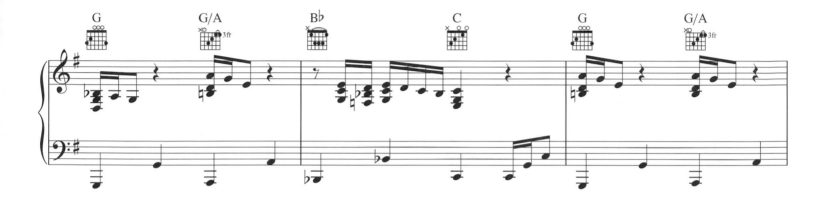

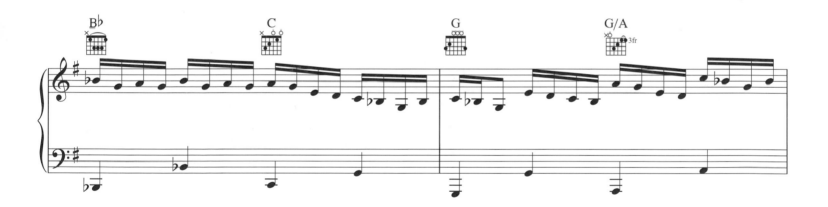

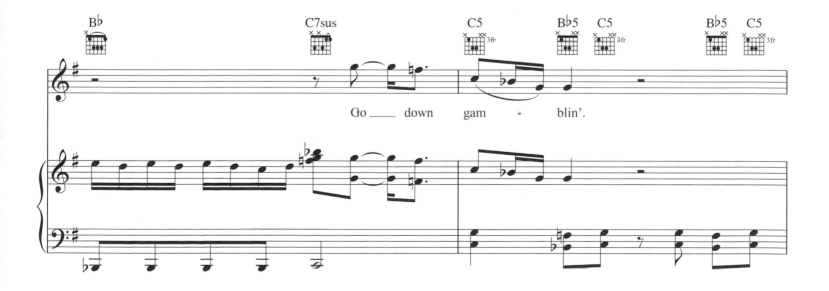

Go ___ down gam - blin'.

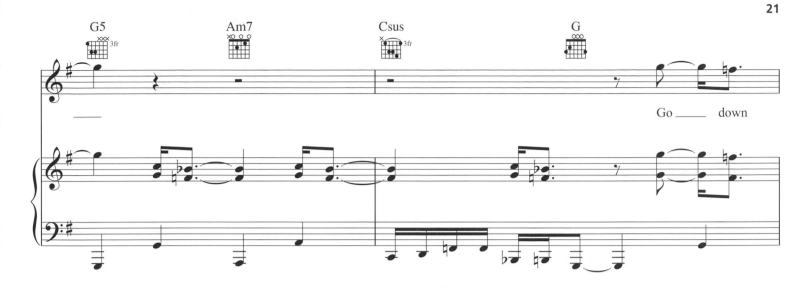

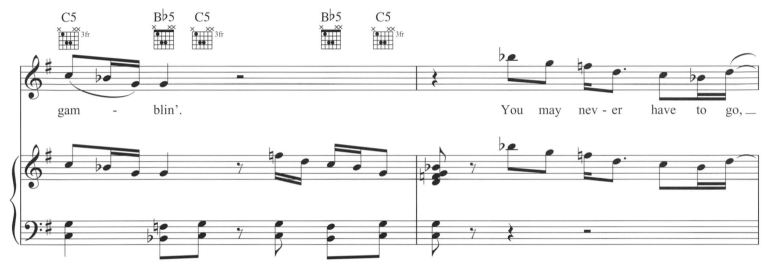

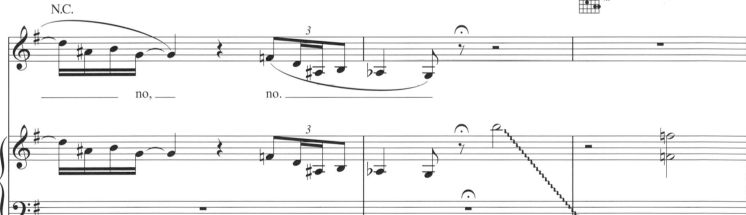

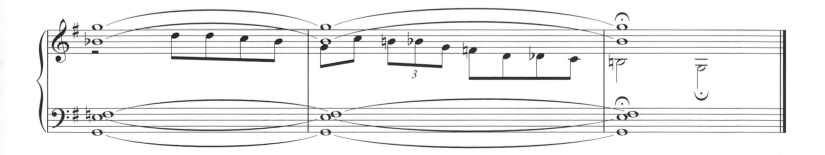

GOD BLESS THE CHILD

Words and Music by ARTHUR HERZOG JR.
and BILLIE HOLIDAY

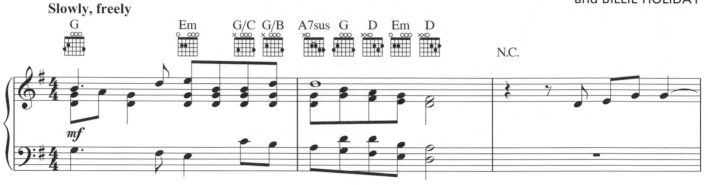

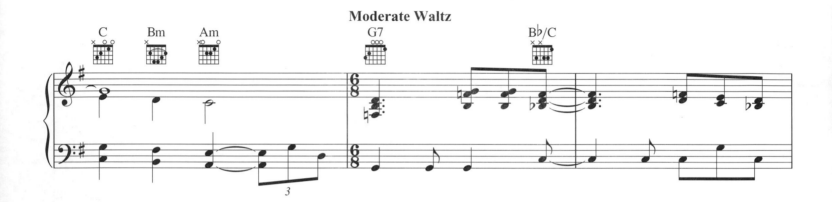

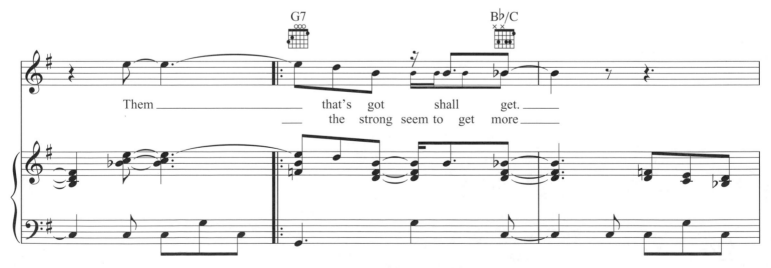

Them ___ that's got shall get. ___
___ the strong seem to get more ___

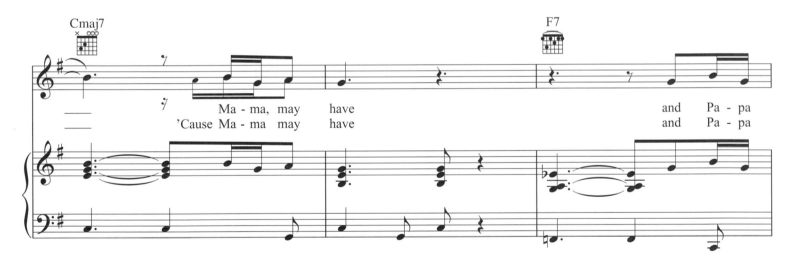

Them that's not shall lose. ____
while the weak ones fade. ____

So the Bi-
Emp-ty pock-

- ble says
- ets don't

and it still is ____ news. ____
ev-er make the ____ grade. ____

Ma-ma, may have
'Cause Ma-ma may have

and Pa-pa
and Pa-pa

may have ____
may have ____

but God bless' the child ____ that's got his
but God bless' the child ____ that's got his

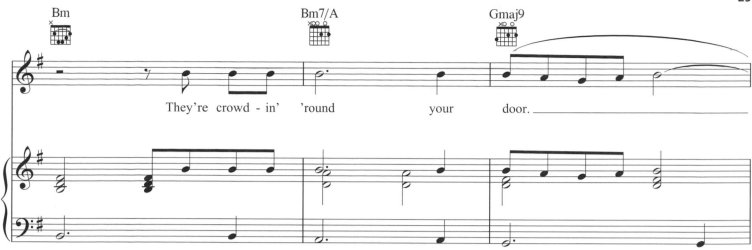

They're crowd - in' 'round your door. _____

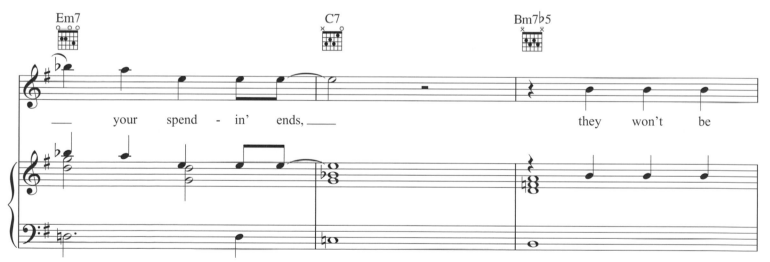

When the mon - ey's gone _____ and all _____

_____ your spend - in' ends, _____ they won't be

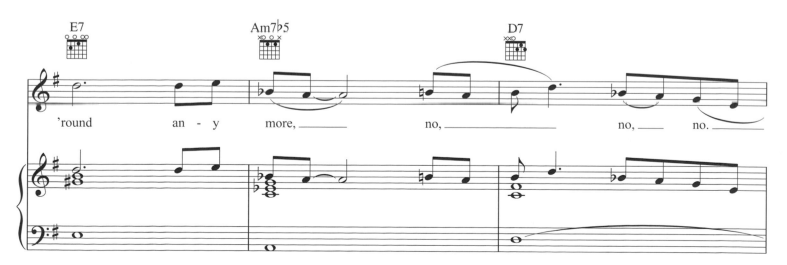

'round an - y more, _____ no, _____ no, _____ no.

Tempo I

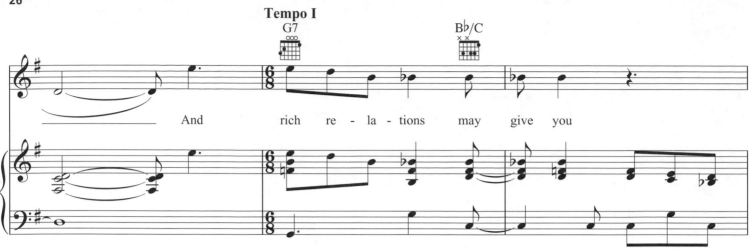

And rich re - la - tions may give you

a crust of bread and such. You can

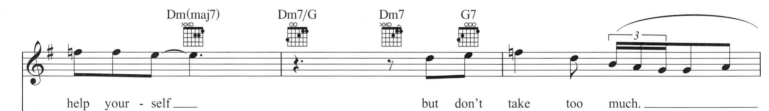

help your - self ___ but don't take too much. ___

Ma - ma may have ___ and

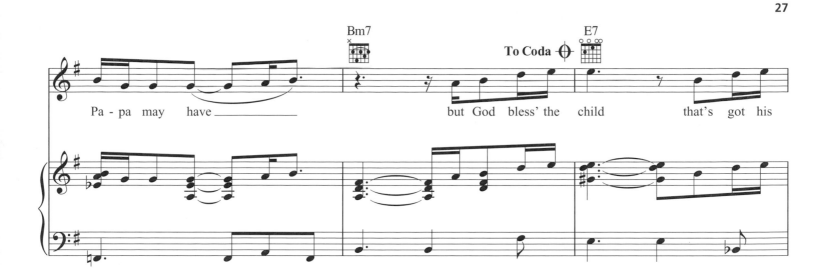

Pa - pa may have _____ but God bless' the child that's got his

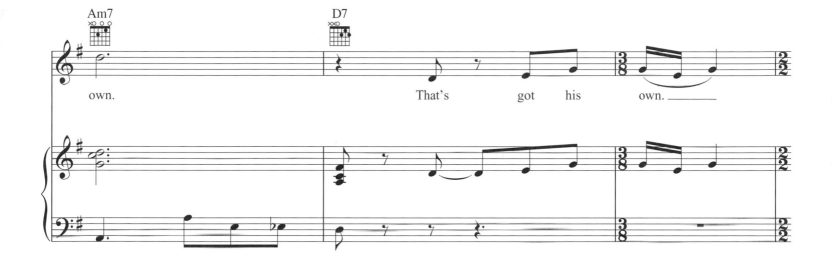

own. That's got his own. _____

Fast Latin in 2

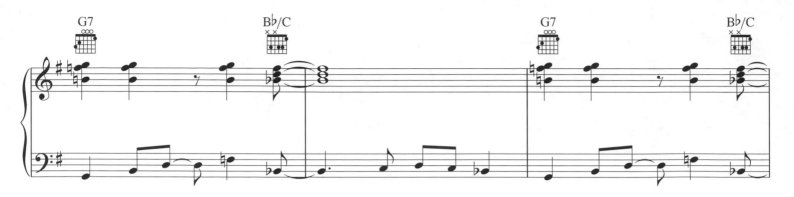

(Instrumental solos ad lib.)

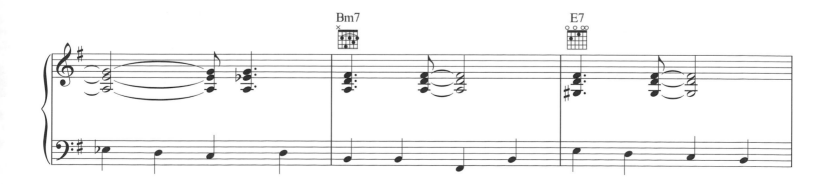

Fast Latin in 2

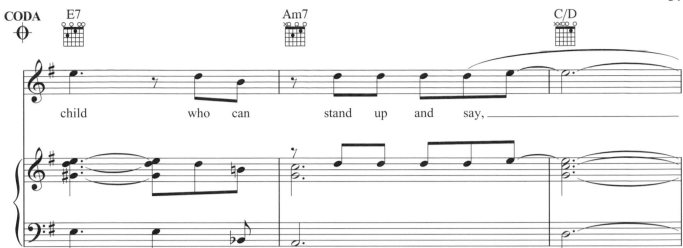

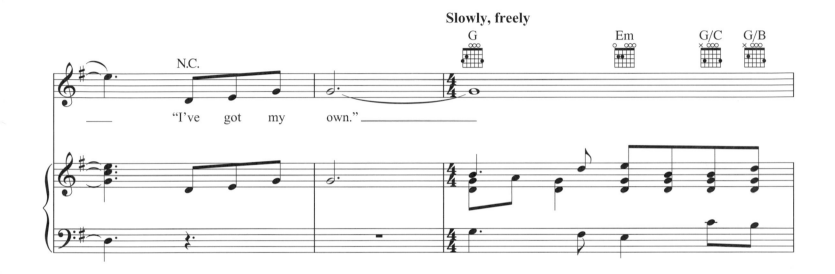

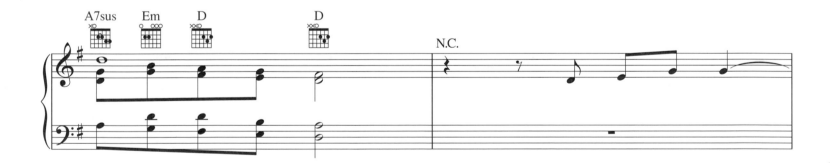

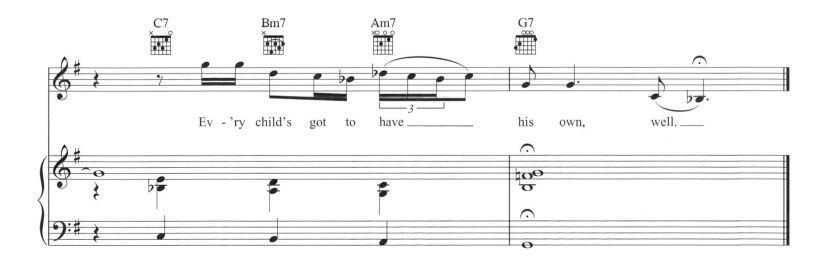

I CAN'T QUIT HER

Words and Music by AL KOOPER
and IRWIN LEVINE

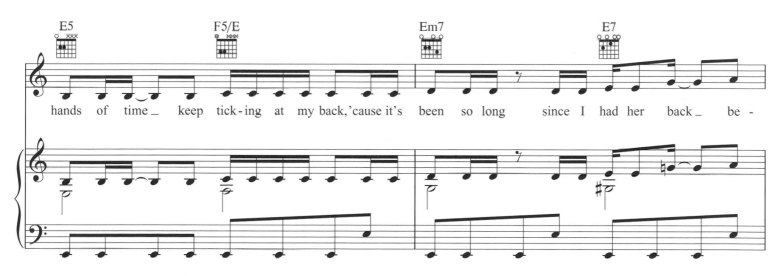

I can't side ___ me,

yeah. ___ True love is some - thing ev - 'ry

young boy knows a - bout, ___ and he fights his whole ___ soul ___ best to

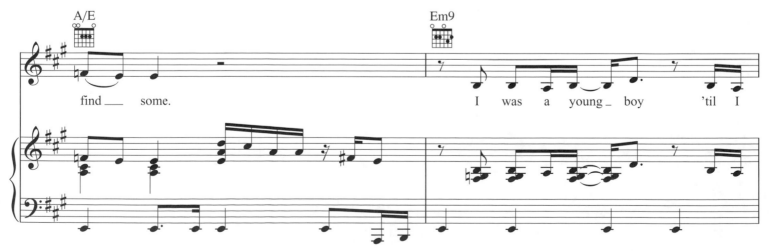

find ___ some. I was a young ___ boy 'til I

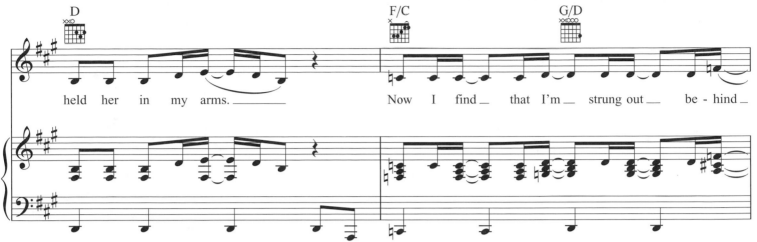

held her in my arms. _____ Now I find_ that I'm_ strung out_ be-hind_

_____ some. _____

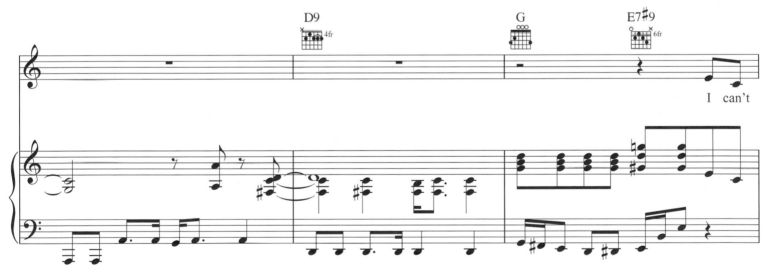

I can't

quit her. She got her hand on me,_ she got a-hold of my soul;_ I can't_

quit her, 'cause I see her face ev-'ry-where I go. I can't

quit her, woo, yeah. I

know, you know I see your face ev-'ry-where I go.

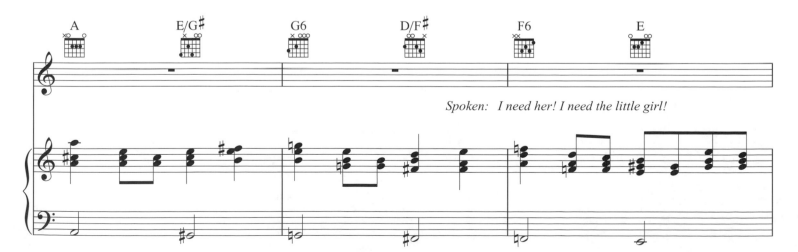

Spoken: I need her! I need the little girl!

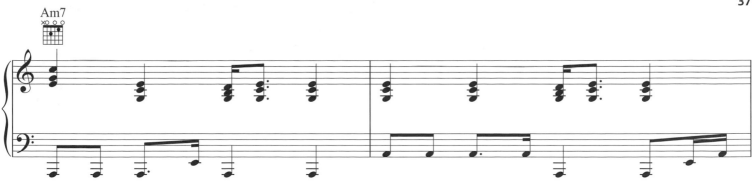

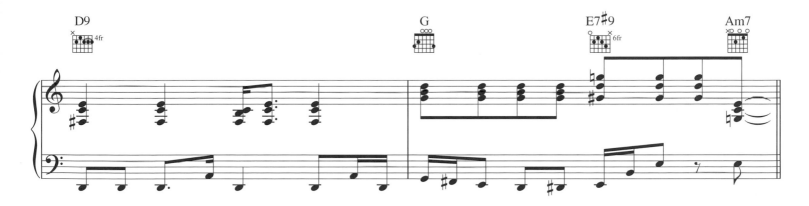

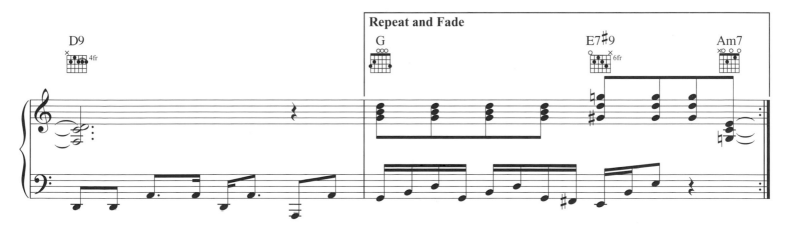

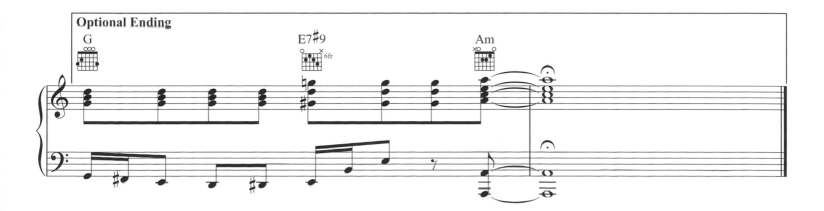

I LOVE YOU MORE THAN YOU'LL EVER KNOW

Words and Music by
AL KOOPER

Moderately slow, in 2

Guitar fills ad lib.

mf

If I ev-er leave you,

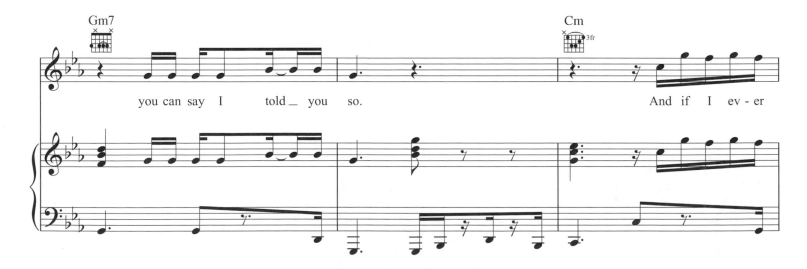

you can say I told __ you so. And if I ev-er

more than you'll ev - er know. __

I'm not try-ing to be an - y kind of

man. __ I'm try-ing to be some - bod - y __

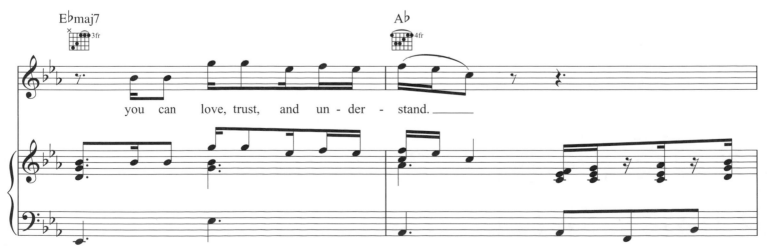

you can love, trust, and un - der - stand. __

I know that I can be, __ yeah, _____ a part of you that no one __

else can see. __ I just got-ta hear, well, hear you say it's al -

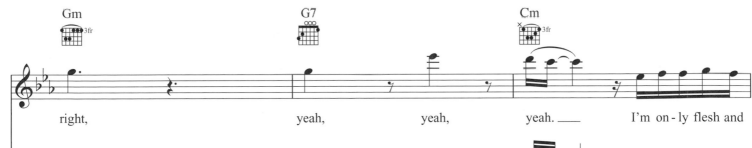

right, yeah, yeah, yeah. __ I'm on - ly flesh and

blood. __ I could be ev -'ry-thing that you de -

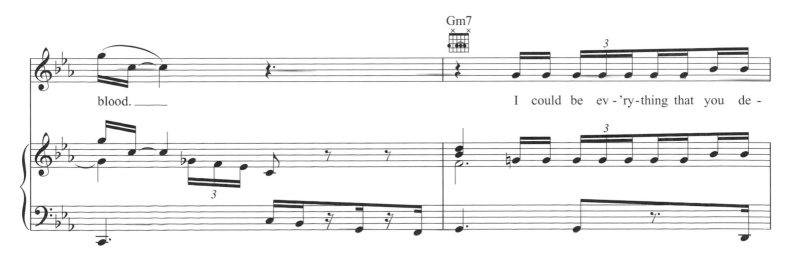

I could be pres - i - dent of Gen - er - al Mo -

tors, ba - by, or just a ti - ny lit - tle grain of sand.

Is that any - y way for a man to ___ car - ry on?

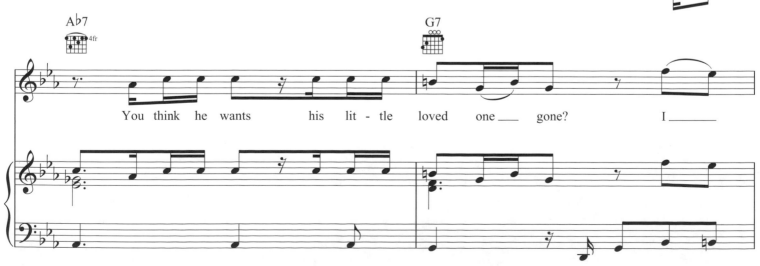

You think he wants his lit - tle loved one ___ gone? I ___

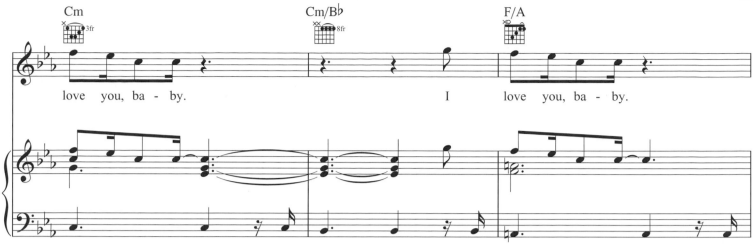

love you, ba - by.   I   love you, ba - by.

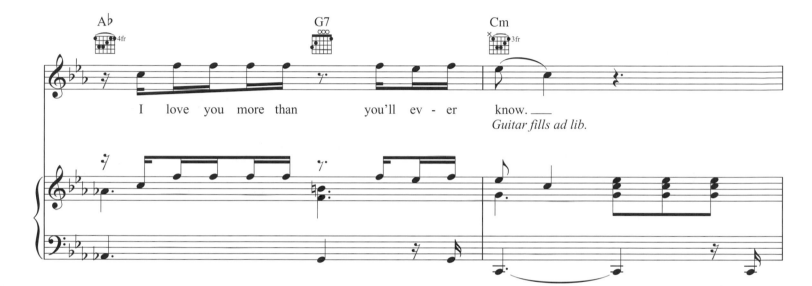

I love you more than   you'll ev - er   know. ___

Guitar fills ad lib.

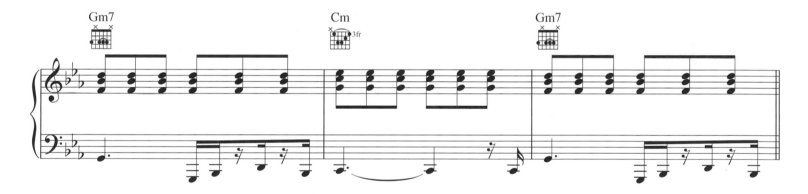

Alto sax solo ad lib.

46

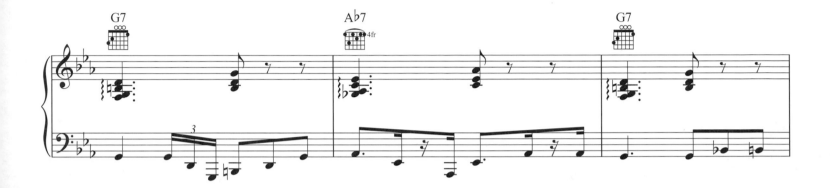

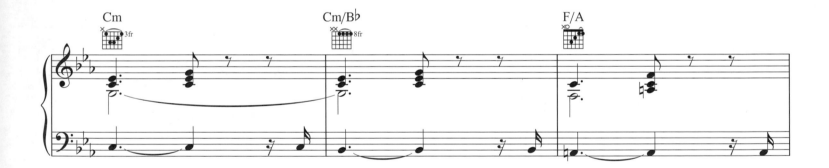

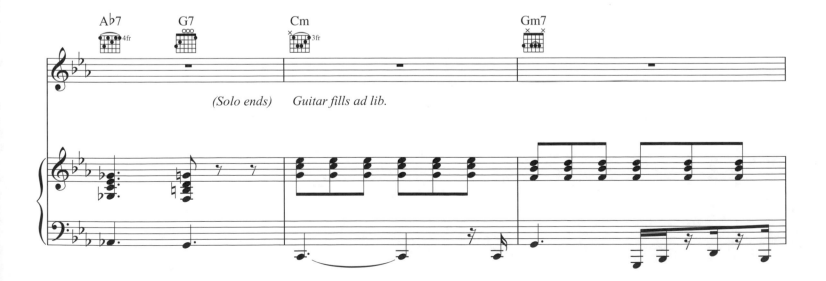

(Solo ends)   *Guitar fills ad lib.*

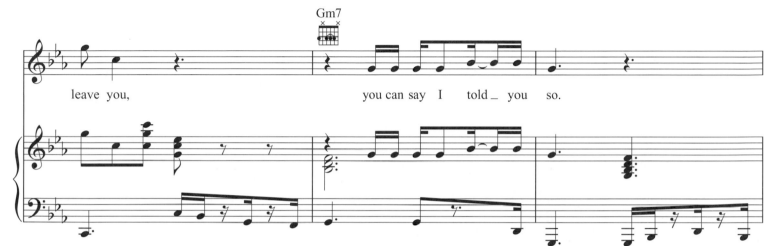

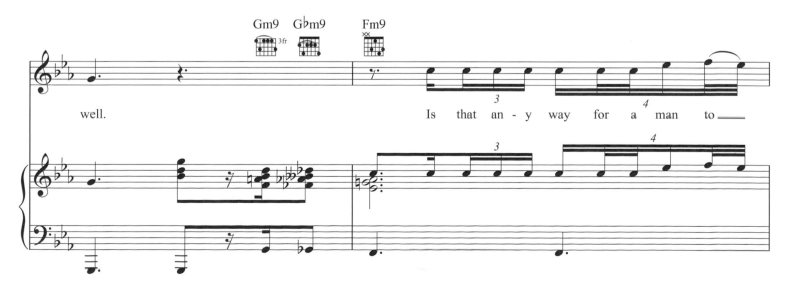

LISA, LISTEN TO ME

Words and Music by DAVID CLAYTON-THOMAS
and DICK HALLIGAN

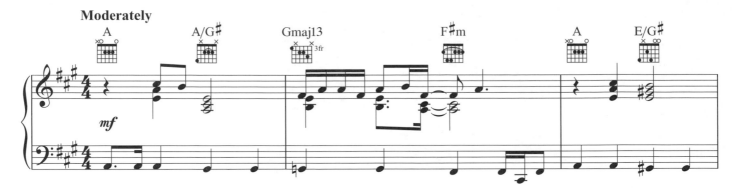

Moderately

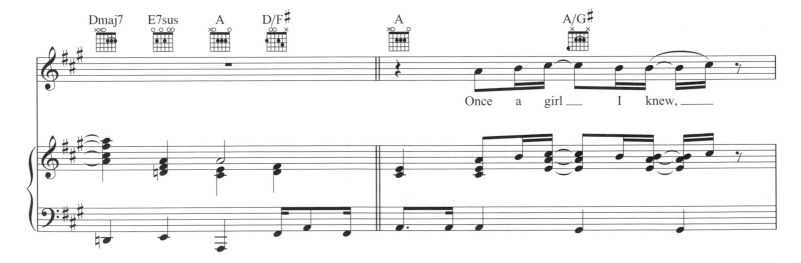

Once a girl ___ I knew, ___

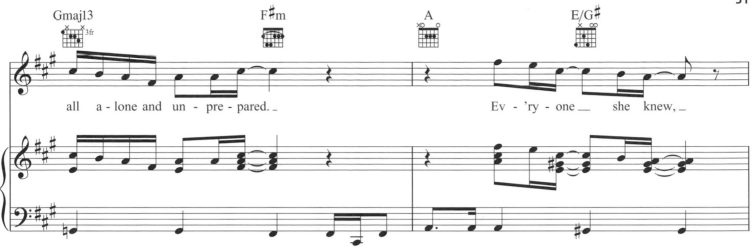

all a-lone and un-pre-pared. _ Ev-'ry-one _ she knew, _

run-ning scared. Then she found _____ him, or

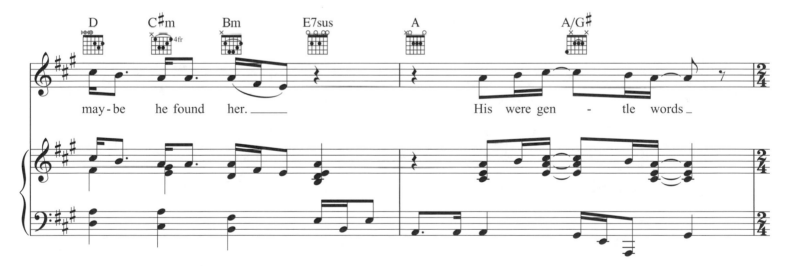

may-be he found her. _____ His were gen-tle words _

she had nev-er heard be-fore. _____ He said,

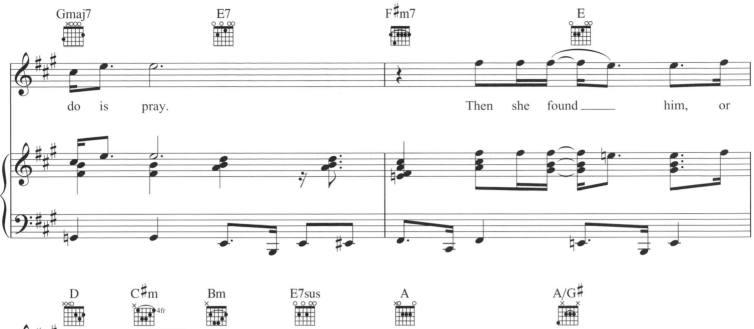

do is pray. Then she found _____ him, or

may-be he found her. _____ His were gen - tle words _

she had nev - er heard be - fore. _ Ooh, _____ well, _____

she had nev - er heard be - fore. _ He said, "Li - sa, lis - ten to me: don't you

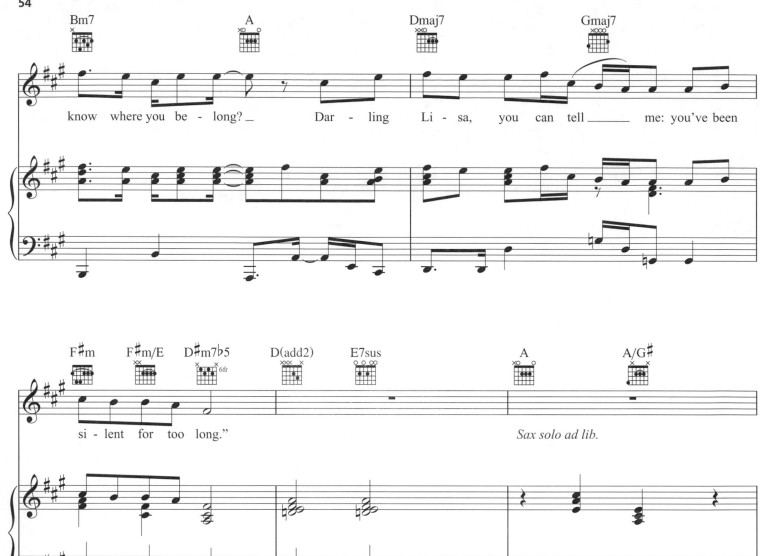

know where you be - long? _ Dar - ling Li - sa, you can tell _____ me: you've been

si - lent for too long."   *Sax solo ad lib.*

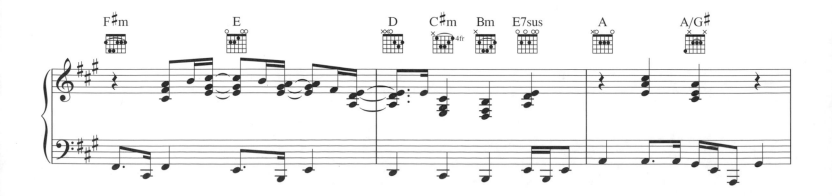

(Solo ends) He said,

"Li - sa, lis - ten to ___ me: don't you know where you be - long? ___ Dar - ling

Li - sa, ___ you can tell me: you've been si - lent for too long."

Once a girl ___ I knew, ___ all a - lone and un - pre - pared. ___

SO LONG, DIXIE

Words and Music by BARRY MANN
and CYNTHIA WEIL

she _____ had you hat - ing to leave.

So long, Dix - ie.

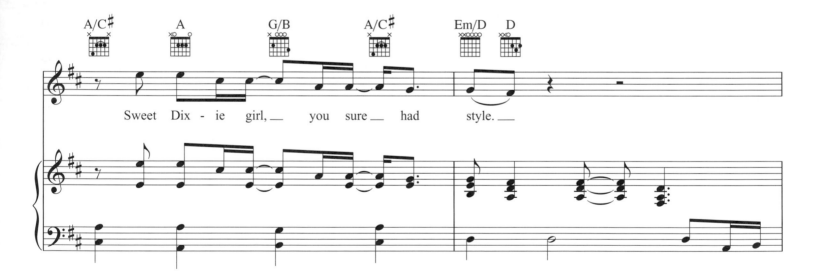

Sweet Dix - ie girl, __ you sure __ had style. __

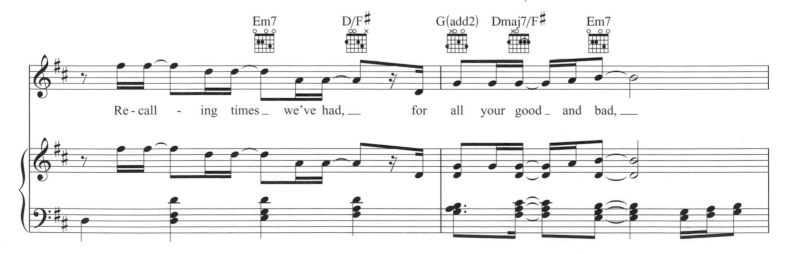

Re - call - ing times __ we've had, __ for all your good __ and bad, __

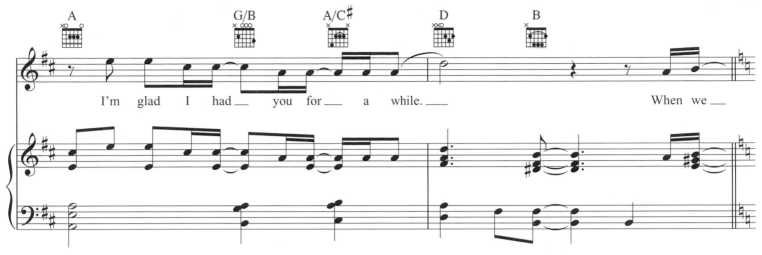

I'm glad I had___ you for___ a while.___ When we___

___ get the blues___ we just___ shine up our shoes___ and head___

___ for Dix-ie's place.___ Ah, we'd

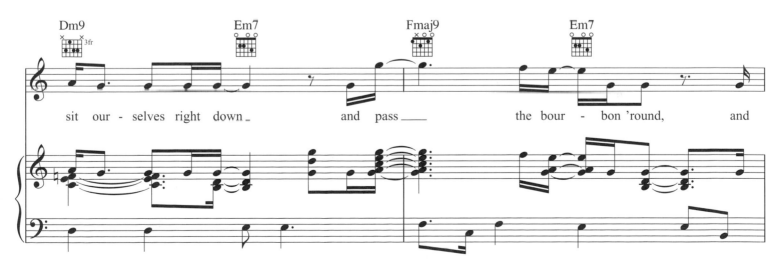

sit our-selves right down___ and pass___ the bour-bon 'round, and

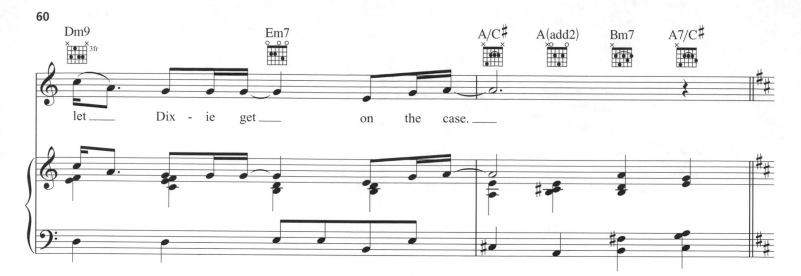

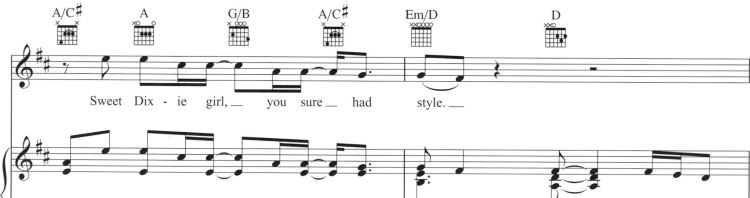

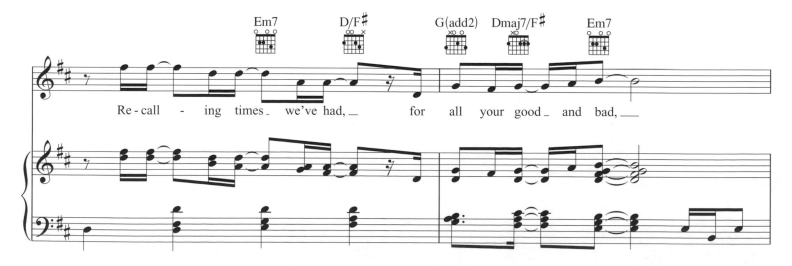

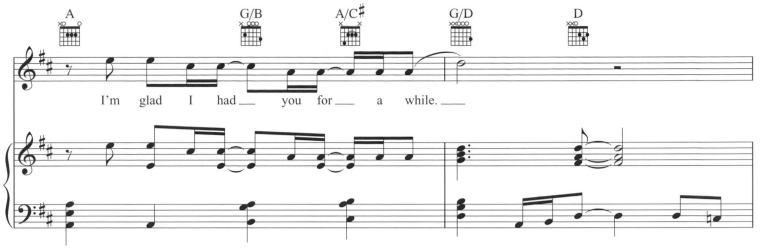

I'm glad I had __ you for __ a while. __

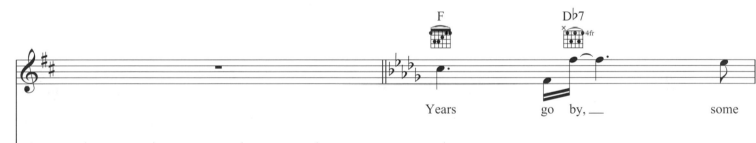

Guitar solo ad lib.

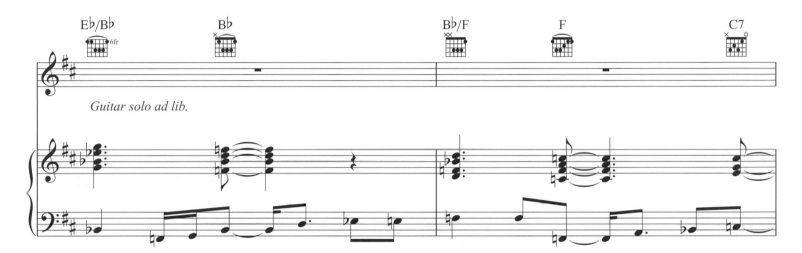

Years go by, __ some

mem-'ries fade and die; __ but Dix - ie, you still shine. __

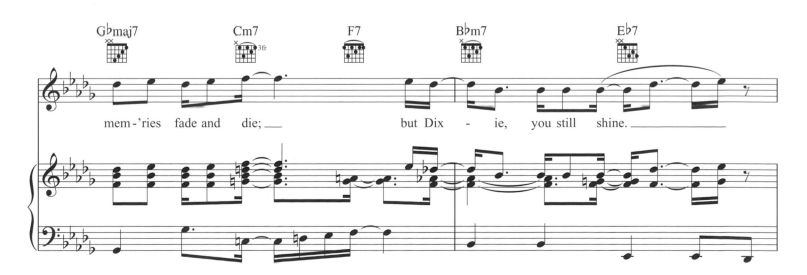

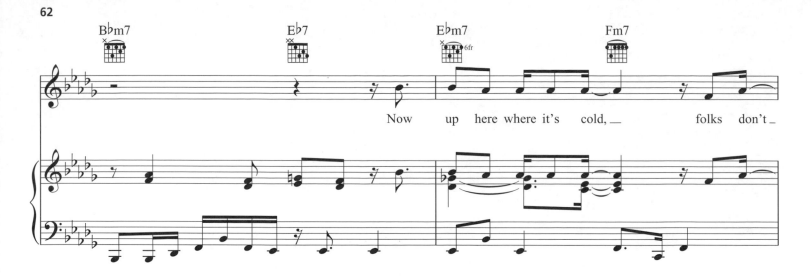

Now up here where it's cold, __ folks don't __

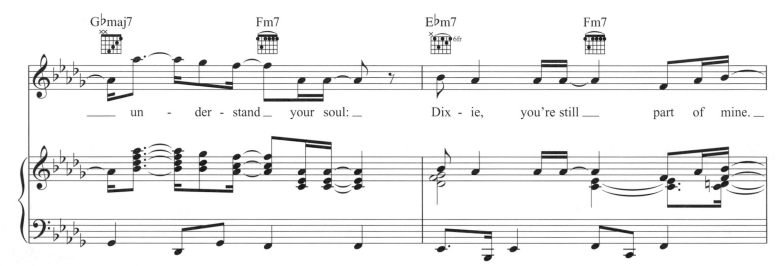

__ un - der - stand __ your soul: __ Dix - ie, you're still __ part of mine. __

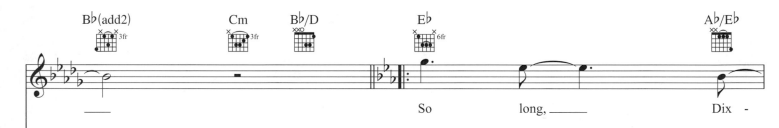

__ So long, _____ Dix -

- ie.   Sweet Dix - ie girl, __ you sure __ had

LUCRETIA MAC EVIL

Words and Music by
DAVID CLAYTON-THOMAS

Hard luck and trou - ble
Back seat De - li - lah,

bound to be your claim to fame. _
that's your sixth big jug of wine, _

_____ wom-an.

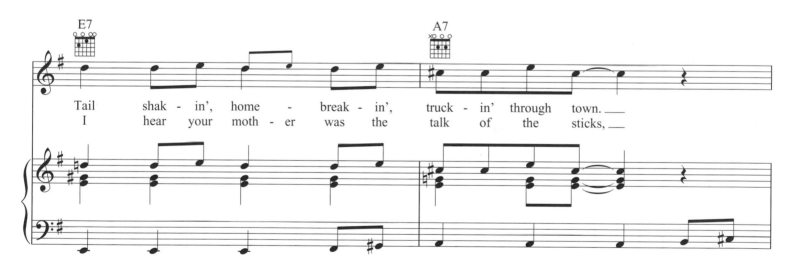

Tail shak - in', home - break - in', truck - in' through town. ___
I hear your moth - er was the talk of the sticks, ___

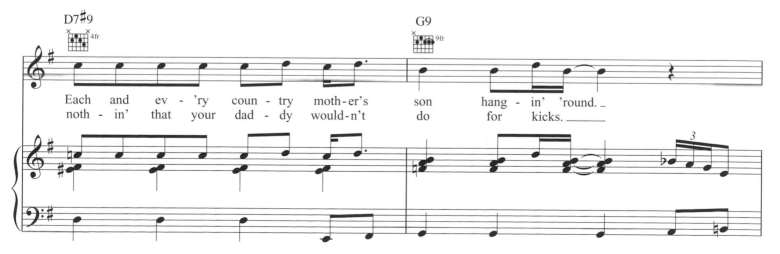

Each and ev - 'ry coun - try moth - er's son hang - in' 'round. __
noth - in' that your dad - dy would - n't do for kicks. ____

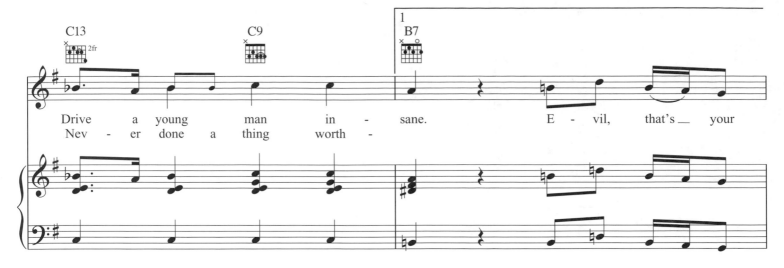

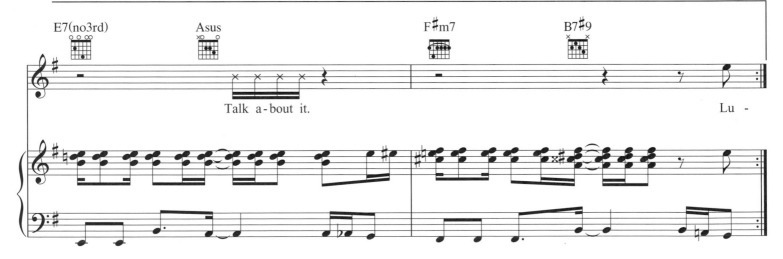

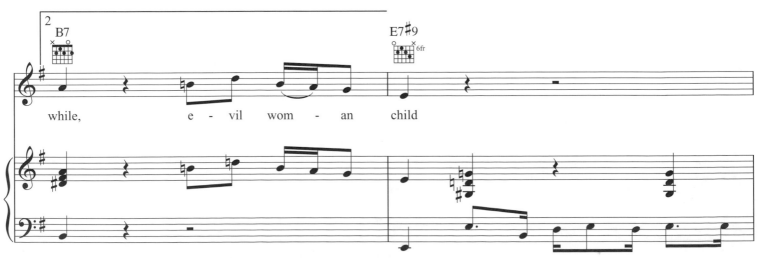

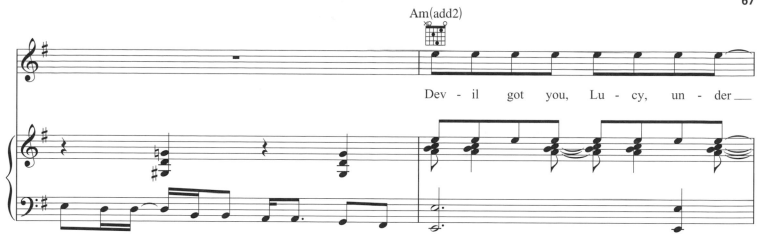

Dev - il got you, Lu - cy, un - der ___

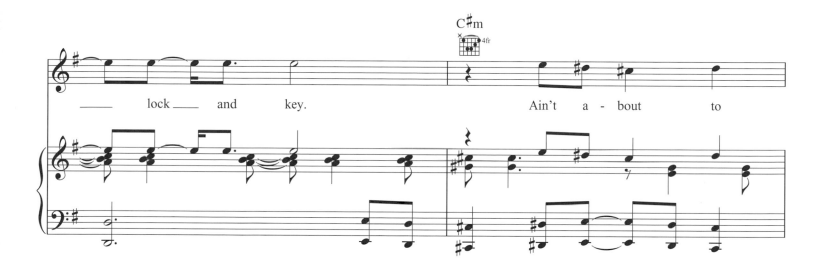

___ lock ___ and key. Ain't a - bout to

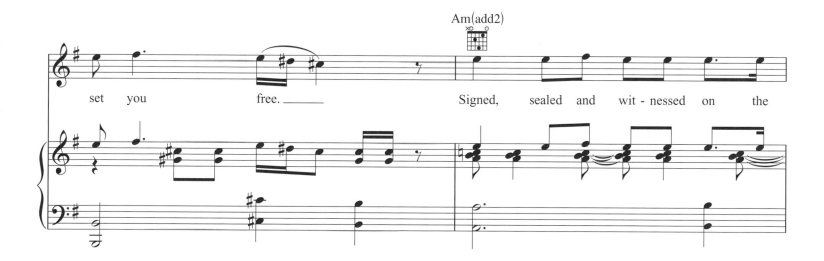

set you free. ___ Signed, sealed and wit - nessed on the

day you were born. No use try - ing to fake ___ him out,

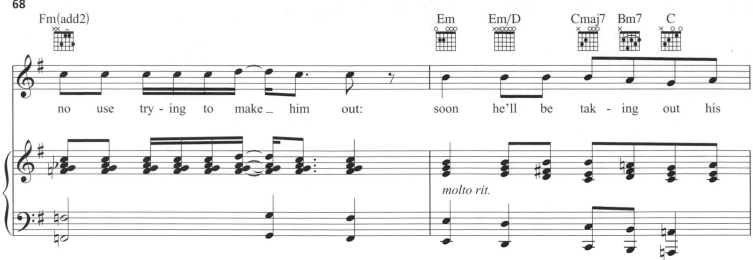

Fm(add2)   Em   Em/D   Cmaj7   Bm7   C

no use try-ing to make _ him out: soon he'll be tak-ing out his

molto rit.

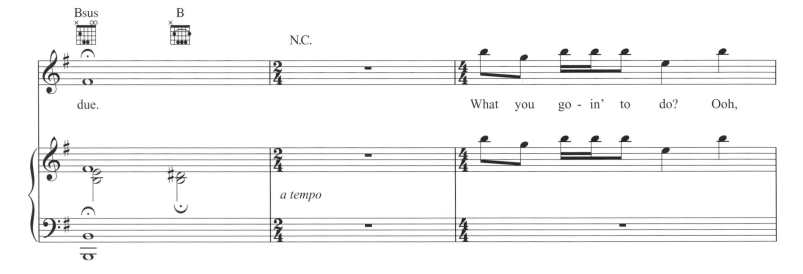

Bsus   B   N.C.

due.   What you go-in' to do? Ooh,

a tempo

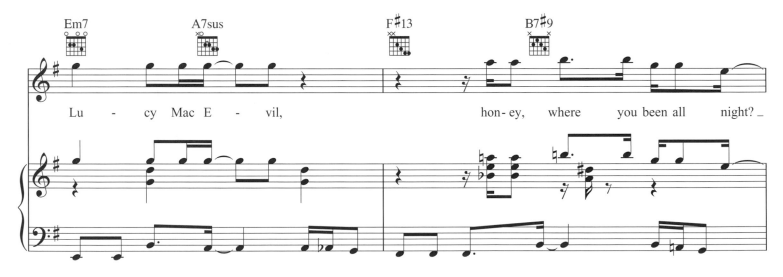

Em7   A7sus   F#13   B7#9

Lu - cy Mac E - vil,   hon-ey, where you been all night? _

Em7   A7sus   F#13   B7#9

Your hair's all messed up, babe, and the clothes you're wear-ing just __ don't fit you

right, __ no.

Dad - dy Joe's pay-ing your month - ly rent, __

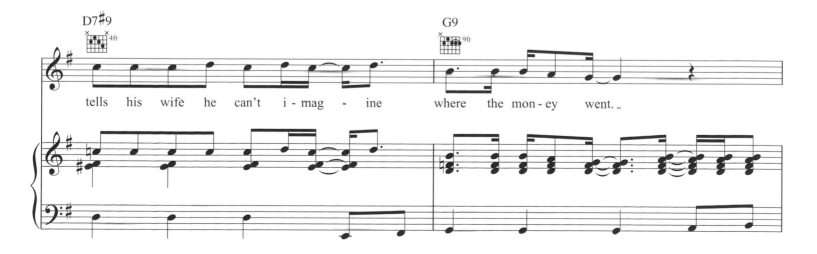

tells his wife he can't i - mag - ine where the mon-ey went. __

Dress - ing you up in style, e - vil wom - an

child.

Spoken: Ooh, Lucy, you just so damn bad!

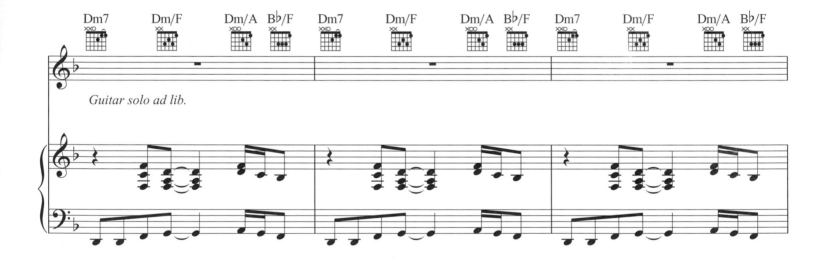

Guitar solo ad lib.

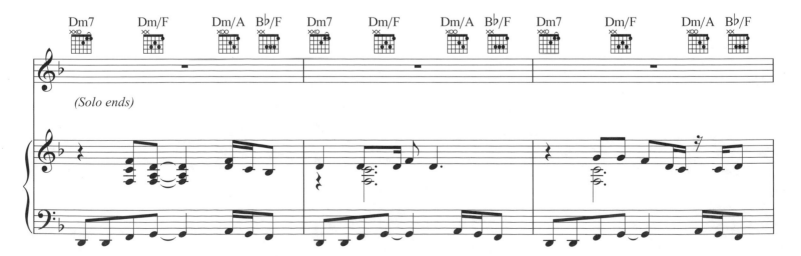

(Solo ends)

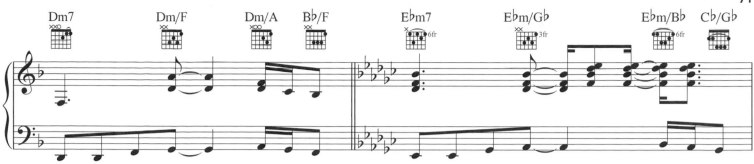

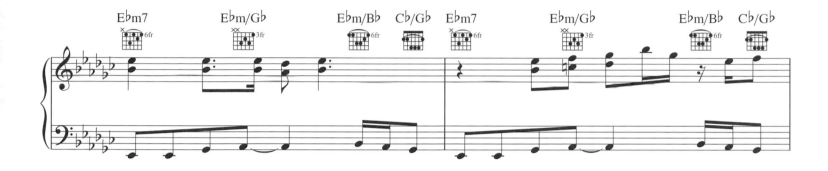

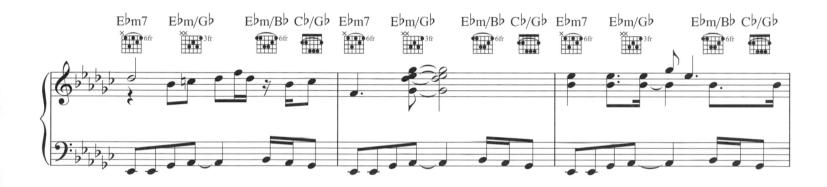

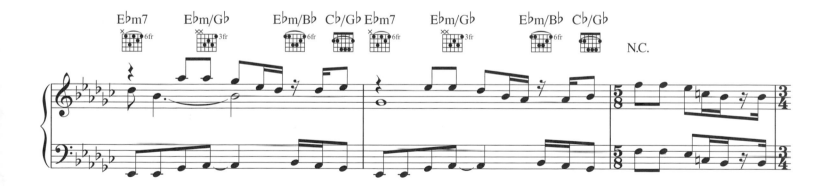

MORE AND MORE

By PEE VEE
and DON JUAN

Moderately fast

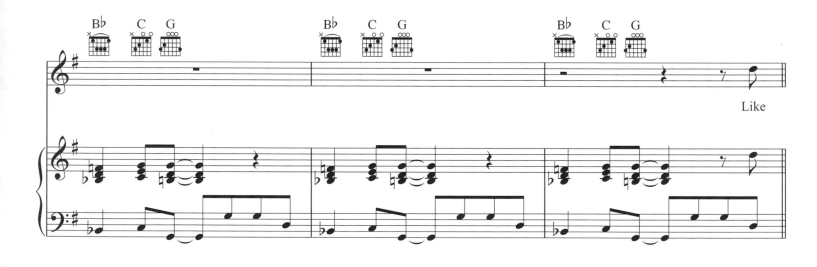

Like

med-i-cine, ba-by, you're good for me.___ Like hon-ey, dar-lin', yeah,___ I

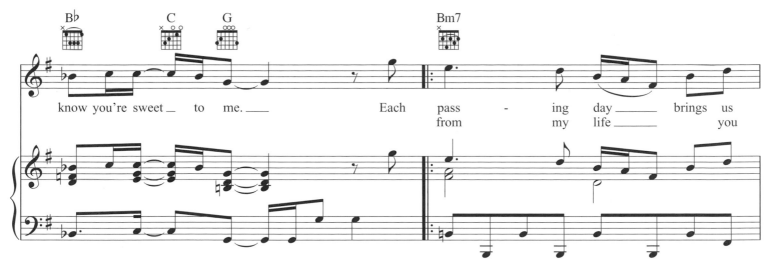

know you're sweet ___ to me. ___ Each pass - - ing day ___ brings us
from my life ___ brings you

much clos - er to - geth - er. And the love you give me, dar - lin', just gets
ev - er de - cide to go, ___ would de - stroy ___ in a sec - ond what took a

bet - ter and bet - ter. ⎫
life - time to mold. ___ ⎬ That's why my love for you ___

keeps on ___ grow - in' more and more ___ all the time. ___

More and more _____ all the time. _

Like a

N.C.

ship that's drift - in', ba - by, you're a - part from _ me. _____ Like old _

___ man time, you con - trol my des - ti - ny. _ If

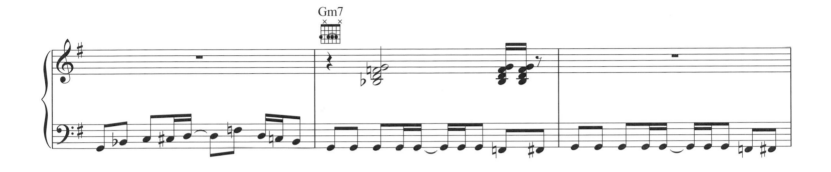

N.C.

Sure as the

sun - rise, _____ I'll stand by your side. _____

Sure as the day - break, _ I'll love you for heav-en's sake. _____

I'm read - y to pay, _ yeah, my dues for lov - in' you. _

For lov-in' you too much, wom-an, you know I stand ac-cused. ___

More, more, all the time. ___ More and more. ___

SOMETIMES IN WINTER

Words and Music by
STEVE KATZ

To Coda ⊕

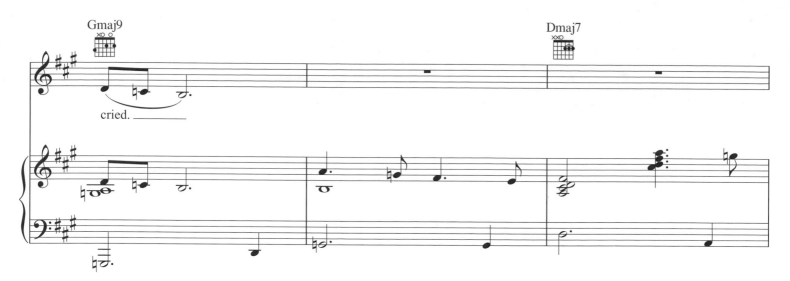

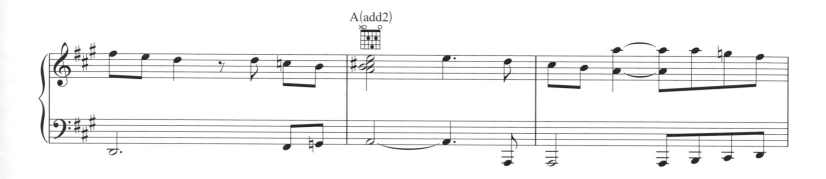

By the win-dow once _____ I wait-ed for you. Laugh-ing slight-ly,

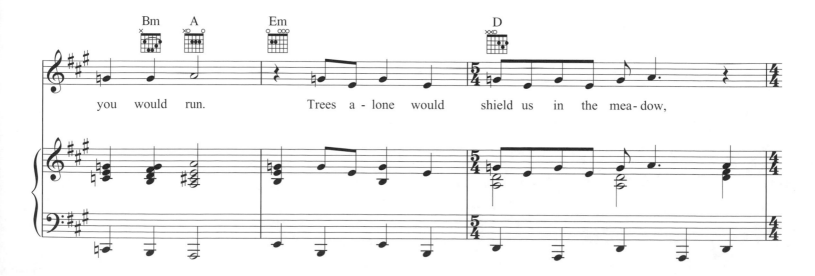

you would run. Trees a-lone would shield us in the mea-dow,

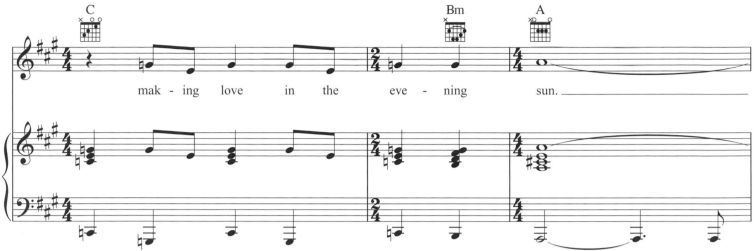

mak - ing love in the eve - ning sun. ___

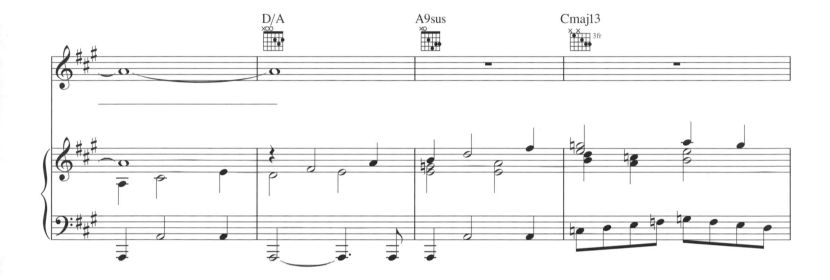

Now you're gone, girl, ___

rit.

a tempo

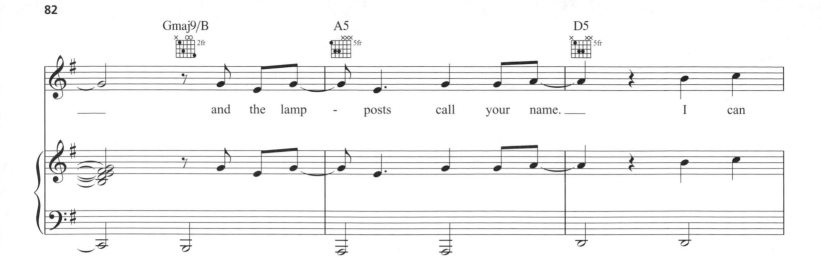

and the lamp - posts call your name. ____ I can

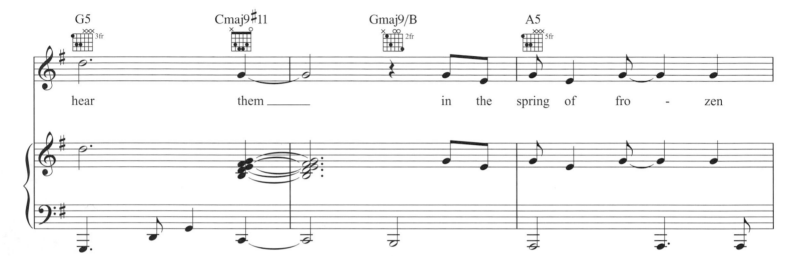

hear them _____ in the spring of fro - zen

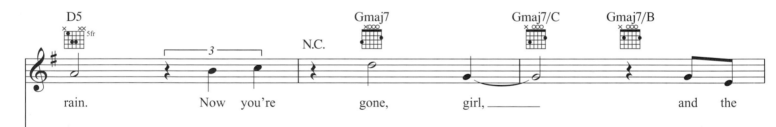

rain. Now you're gone, girl, _____ and the

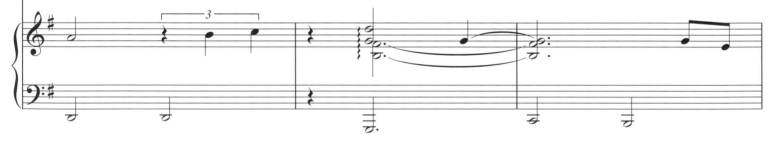

time's slowed down 'til dawn. It's a cold room, ____

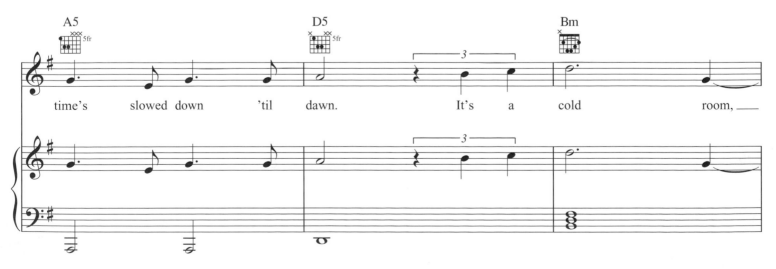

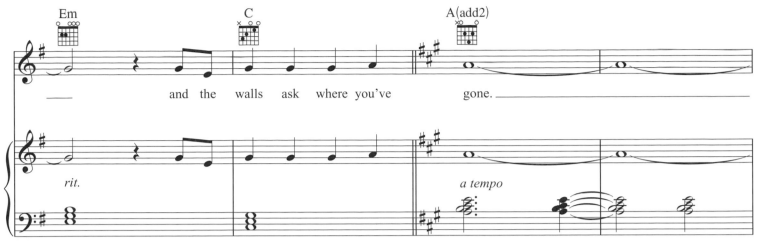

and the walls ask where you've gone.

rit.

a tempo

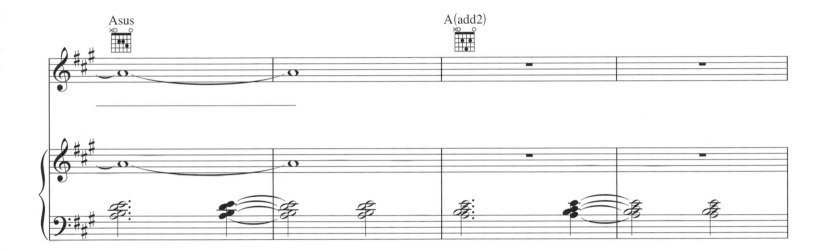

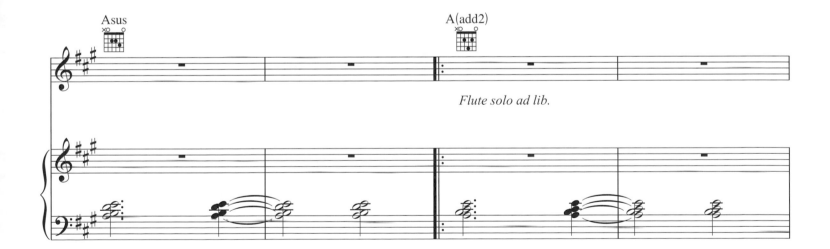

Flute solo ad lib.

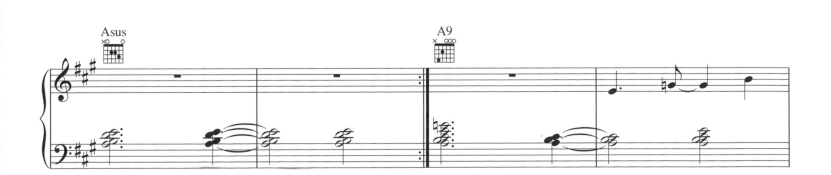

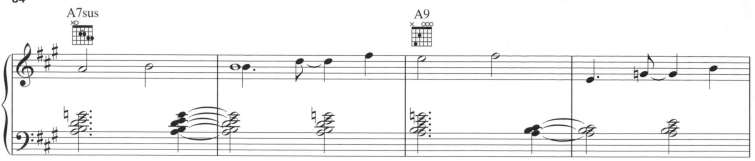

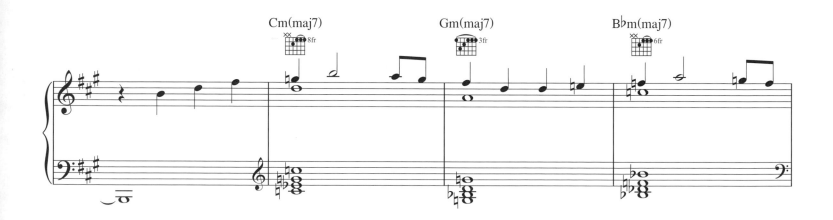

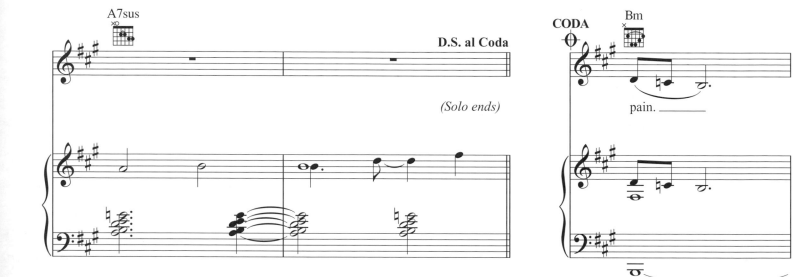

YOU'VE MADE ME SO VERY HAPPY

Words and Music by BERRY GORDY, FRANK E. WILSON,
BRENDA HOLLOWAY and PATRICE HOLLOWAY

You treat-ed me so kind, _ I'm a-bout to lose _ my mind. _ You made me _ so

ver - y hap - py. I'm so glad you came in - to my _

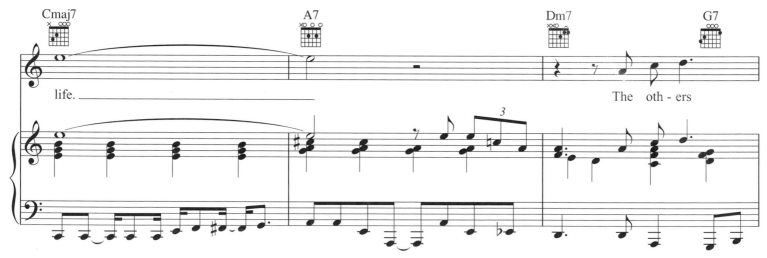

life. _ The oth - ers

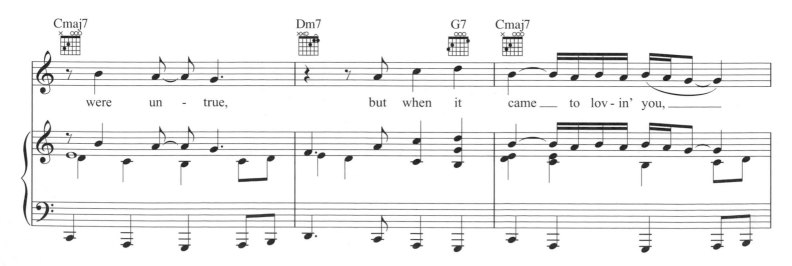

were un - true, but when it came _ to lov - in' you, _

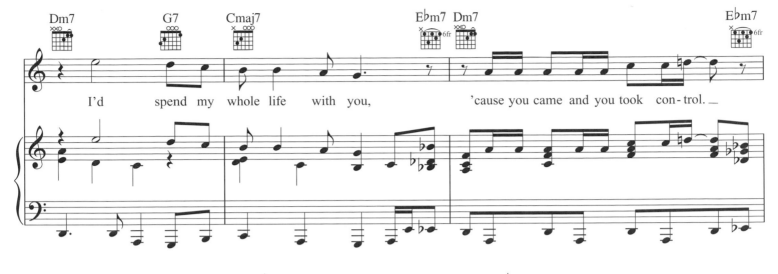

I'd spend my whole life with you, 'cause you came and you took con-trol. _

You touched my ver-y soul. _ You al-ways showed me that _ lov-ing you is where it's at.

You made me _ so ver-y hap-py. I'm so glad you

came in-to my _ life.

Thank you, ba - by! __

Yeah, yeah.

I love you so much, it seems___ you're e - ven in my dreams.__ I can

hear,____ ba - by, I __ can hear you're call - ing me.

I'm so in love with you ____ all I ev - er want to do ____ is

thank you, ba - by, thank you, ba - by!

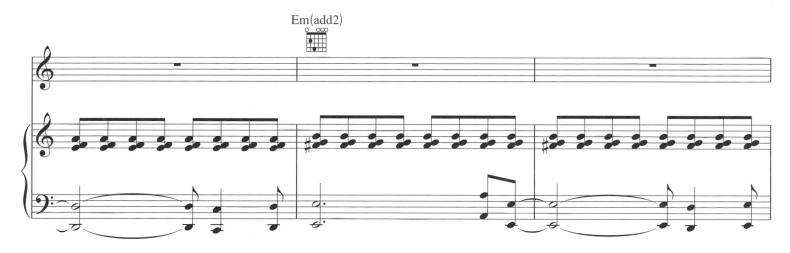

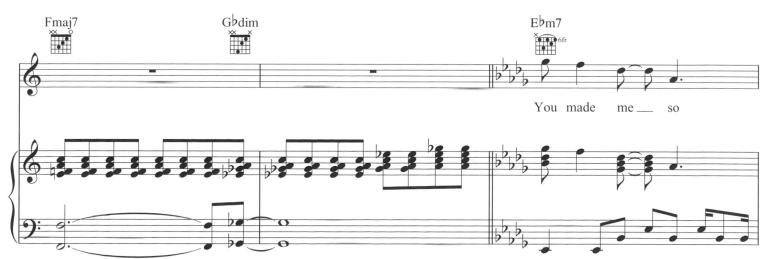

You made me ____ so

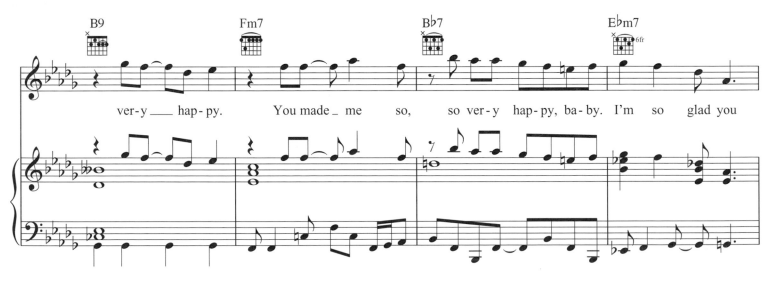

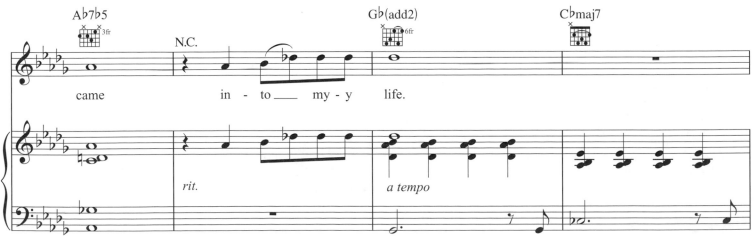

Mmm, _____ I wan-na thank you, girl! Ev-'ry

day of my life _____ I wan-na thank you. You made me so __

_____ ver-y hap-py. Oh, I wan-na spend my life __ thank-ing you. __ Thank you,

Repeat and Fade | **Optional Ending**

ba - by! __ Thank you, ba - by! ____ Thank you, ba - by!

SPINNING WHEEL

Words and Music by
DAVID CLAYTON-THOMAS

You got no mon- ey, you got no home, ___ spin-ning wheel

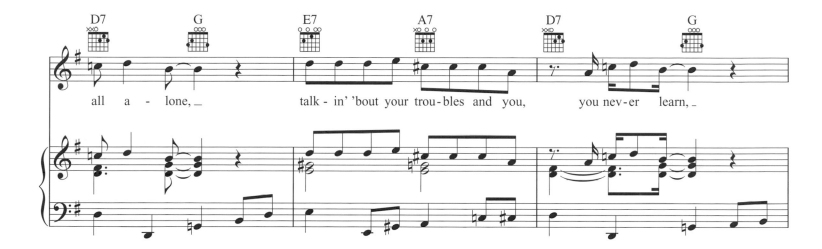

all a - lone, ___ talk- in' 'bout your trou-bles and you, you nev-er learn, ___

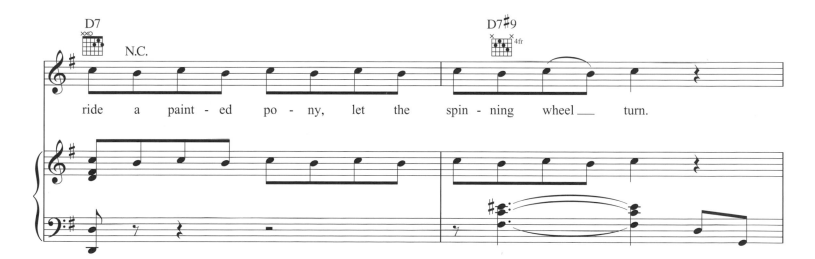

ride a paint - ed po- ny, let the spin-ning wheel ___ turn.

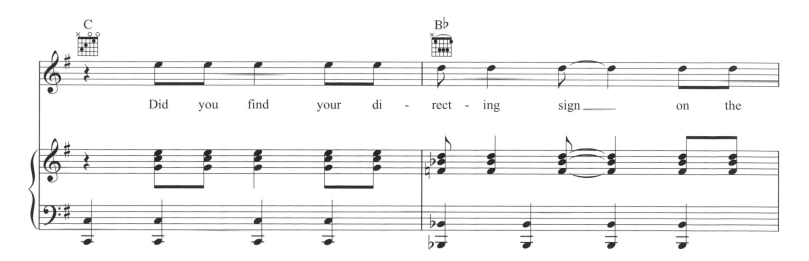

Did you find your di - rect - ing sign ___ on the

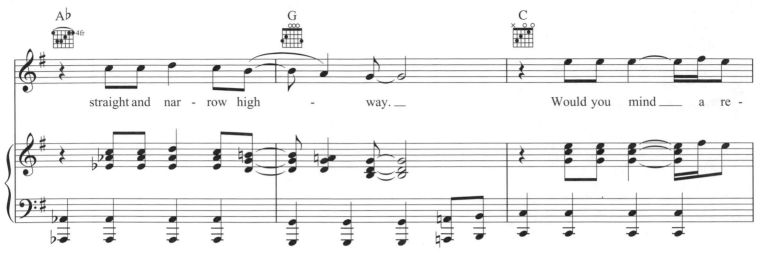

straight and nar - row high - way. __ Would you mind __ a re-

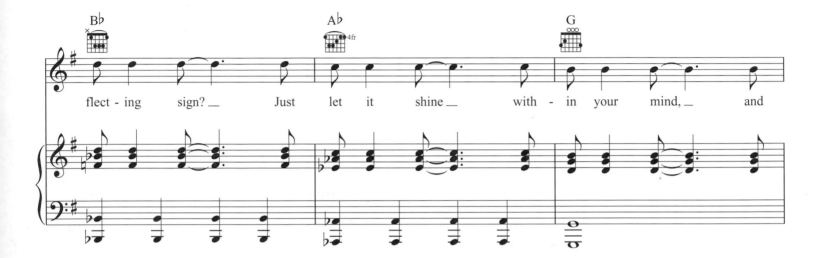

flect - ing sign? __ Just let it shine __ with - in your mind, __ and

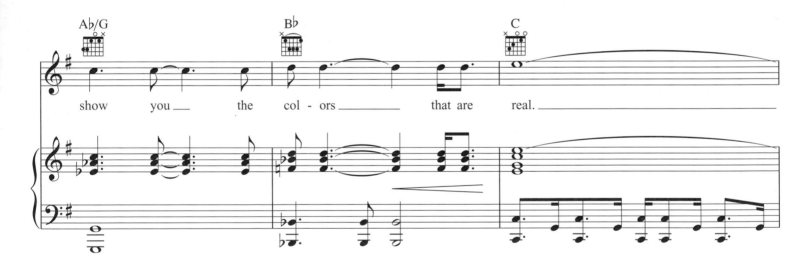

show you __ the col - ors __ that are real. __

Some - one is wait - ing just for you, ___ spin - ning wheel

spin - ning true. ___ Drop all your trou - bles by the riv - er - side, ___

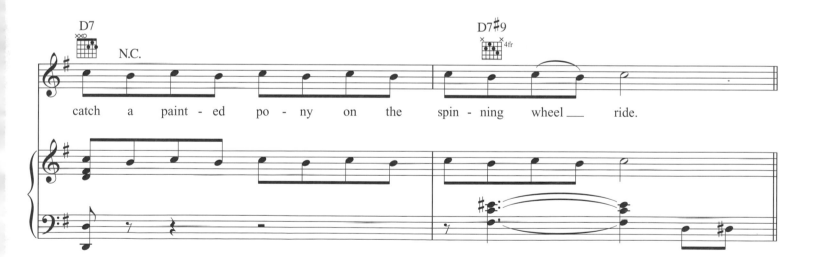

catch a paint - ed po - ny on the spin - ning wheel ___ ride.

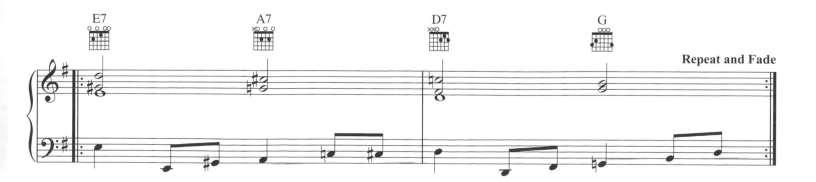

Repeat and Fade